HI BEAUTIFUL

A LETTER FOR SOMEONE YOU LOVE

Andy Painter and Bill Gaiennie

SPARK Publications
Charlotte, North Carolina

Hi Beautiful
A Letter for Someone You Love

Andy Painter and Bill Gaiennie

Designed, produced, and published by
SPARK Publications
SPARKpublications.com
Charlotte, North Carolina

Stock Image Credit: ArtDesign Illustration / shutterstock.com

Printed in the United States of America

Paperback, July 2023, ISBN: 978-1-953555-60-1
Hardback, July 2023, ISBN: 978-1-953555-59-5
Library of Congress Control Number: 2023912471

 DEDICATION

To all the mothers, fathers, sons, and daughters: may this letter and book inspire you and unleash your spirit to the world.

ACKNOWLEDGMENTS

I would like to acknowledge Bill for writing the beautiful letter that inspired me to write this book.

I wish to express my gratitude to Jessica Gaiennie for allowing me to share Bill's letter with the world. I hope this book honors the love Bill shared for Jess, Gwen, Roxy, Kelly, and Cris and brings him back to each of them when they need him most.

I wish to acknowledge my family, Marianne, Grace, AJ, and Avery. Each of you inspire me to be a better version of myself every day, and I hope I can always do the same for you.

I would like to honor Steve Davis for being a true partner to me and Bill. I would also like to acknowledge the entire Davisbase family for celebrating and honoring Bill in those last years.

A special thank you to Bill's family and friends who share sunset pictures to honor Bill and connect with Bill's spirit every week. Those pictures have inspired me through the years, and the cover of this book is a special acknowledgment of Bill's spirit and the connection we continue to carry forward. A special thanks to my daughter Grace for design and inspiration for the book cover to visually capture this spirit.

I would like to acknowledge those who have given me feedback along this journey, especially Harvey Smith, Elena Jennings, Gareth Kemp, Christine Kinney, Christy Clement, Neville Poole, and Fabi Preslar.

TABLE
OF
CONTENTS

LETTER TO GWEN

"ALL EXISTING MEANS TO YOUR DESIRED END ARE WRONG. THEY ARE NOT YOURS. AND ONLY YOURS IS RIGHT. FOR YOU. CHERISH YOUR ORIGINALITY.

"QUESTION HOW MUCH FREEDOM YOUR PATH AFFORDS YOU. BE UTTERLY RUTHLESS ABOUT IT."

DON'T BE A PROBLEM SOLVER. ALONE. THE RESULT OF A SUCCESSFUL PROBLEM SOLVER IS AN ABSENCE OF A PROBLEM, NOTHING MORE. CHANGE & CREATE.

> "NEVER COMPARE YOUR INSIDE WITH SOMEBODY ELSE'S OUTSIDE."

▷ THERE ARE NO SHORTCUTS IN LIFE. BARS, RESTAURANTS, & CLUBS ARE AWASH WITH THOSE WORKING IN A JOB SIMPLY TO SUPPORT MORE TIME WAITING FOR THEIR BIG BREAK.

Bill's original notes in drafting his "A Letter to My Daughter Gwen" post.

BILL'S GIFT

An Introduction

There is no better way to honor my dear friend Bill Gaiennie than to share with you a very thoughtful and significant letter he wrote. The best parts of this book are Bill's direct words and his spirit.

Bill, Steve, and I were business partners in an Agile coaching and training company, Davisbase Consulting. Bill would often write his thoughts about Agile and business on his blog, *The Agile Advisors*. In anticipation of the birth of his daughter, Bill wrote a blog article titled "A Letter to My Daughter Gwen," which he posted on September 5, 2010. This blog is no longer active, so I reposted it to my personal blog on August 29, 2014, to make sure it was never lost. I wanted to make sure it stayed around for both Gwen and his youngest daughter, Roxy. Bill Gaiennie was my friend and my business partner. He passed away on Saturday, August 23, 2014, after battling brain cancer for almost a year. I could share many stories about how amazing Bill was as a writer, speaker, husband, father, son, and friend to so many of us. Instead, I'll share Bill's own words to reveal how amazing he was.

Bill was such a prolific and passionate writer. This letter is one of his best writings and my personal favorite. If you have children, or if you are a son or a daughter, this letter is for you. From the first time I read it and every time I reread it, it impacts me in ways I could have never imagined. I think you'll find it quite special. After you read the letter in this book, I'll share some of the ways it impacted me and ways for you to share it with those you love and cherish.

I hope reading his words and hearing about my experience with this letter will have as much impact on you as Bill and this letter have had on me.

SECTION
ONE

BILL'S LETTER

This blog is typically about all things Agile, but I am taking a slight detour on this post in anticipation of my very first child's birth. Gwendolyn Reece Gaiennie is due to be born on October 7, 2010, and I wanted to share with her future self some things I have learned as I myself grew into adulthood. And if you think that this has nothing to do with business, then you might need to read this yourself.

A LETTER TO MY DAUGHTER GWEN

September 5th, 2010

by Bill Gaiennie

HI BEAUTIFUL,

I may not always be there for you—in fact, no one will. Sad, I know, but you already know this. But *you* will always be with *you*, and because I know you are an intelligent young lady, I wanted to share with you some of the things that I have learned, have been taught, or have picked up along the way. Take these with you as you travel your path through life and look for bits of wisdom you can add so that someday you might also take the opportunity to pass along what you have learned to your own children.

LEAD YOUR LIFE
BASED ON YOUR VALUES.

By the time you read this you can trust that
your values are there, you just may not know
what they are yet. That's ok, so long as you
place importance in identifying them as you
venture into adulthood. Search for them,
be relentless. Know what you will stand
for, and invest your spirit in knowing what
you will *not* stand for. Never seek to please
another person in a quest to satisfy their
values, for when you do, you will likely do
so while sacrificing your own. It took your
father too many years to realize that a life
lived based on anything other than your
values is one spent in a futile attempt to gain
acceptance from another person in an effort
to validate yourself. You don't need to do this;
it is momentarily satisfying and ultimately
vacuous. You matter, because you are *you*.

ALL EXISTING MEANS TO YOUR DESIRED END ARE WRONG.

Another person's path is not yours. And only your path is right. For you. Cherish your originality. Too much stock is put into fitting in, but the truly great ones among us seek to stand up in the current; they choose to stand rather than simply float along with the drift. I know the pressures to be accepted can be overwhelming, but never believe that simply doing what others do is the ultimate value to be had. What do you truly seek in life, Gwen? It is a big question, but one worth asking. And asking again. I allowed too many years to pass before realizing that there is more to life than what can be bought with money. Find what you seek and be open that what you want may not be easy or even immediately possible, but don't allow that to sap you of energy. This is the only life you get; spend it wisely.

THERE ARE NO SHORTCUTS IN LIFE.

I wish this weren't the case, but it is. It just is. The truly amazing things to be had on this earth are gained through hard work, driven by experiences, checkered with failures, but ultimately realized through perseverance. There will be those that try to sell you the easy way out of your problems or the quick path to your goals, and they will be persuasive, but they will be selling you something that simply doesn't exist. Life is not meant to only provide enjoyable experiences, but also suffering, hardships, and pain as well. But this is no mistake, it is by design. A *beautiful* design. These challenging experiences need to be valued as highly as your achievements, for without these you would not appreciate the magnificence of your triumphs. Always remember that you cannot appreciate the mountains if you never experience the valleys.

NEVER COMPARE YOUR INSIDE WITH SOMEBODY ELSE'S OUTSIDE.

As you grow up, you will be bombarded with the message that your value is contingent upon your compliance with another's definition of acceptable. I can only beg of you to not fall for this; it only ends in pain, anguish, and a feeling of being inadequate. You are amazing, so long as you live your life based on the values that you define. Nothing is so important as knowing which principles are worth standing for.

AVOID THE BORING PEOPLE.

Those people that like to play it safe have nothing to offer you; don't waste your time trying to get them to feel your passion. These folks value complacency and sameness as a means for security but in exchange must sacrifice the possibility of something better. *The possibility*. What beautiful words! In fact, new rule: if you ever find someone that is perpetually afraid to do something different simply for the fact that it is different, share your view that there is beauty in risk, but don't dwell on it. If they can't see it, move on. Quickly.

NEVER DO ANYTHING SOLELY ON THE ASSUMPTION THAT YOU WILL BE REWARDED FOR IT.

Your dad is still trying to learn this very valuable lesson. When we act only motivated by the reward given by another, we give away all of our creative power to someone else. Do what *you* believe is right. And remember, the more talented, the more gifted, the more self-motivated a person is, the less they need the props from someone else. You may be your biggest critic, but remember that you also *must* be your biggest cheerleader. You will never need someone else to complete you. You are already whole.

**THE MOST IMPORTANT LESSON I COULD
EVER LEAVE FOR YOU WOULD BE THIS
. . .**

YOU ARE RESPONSIBLE
FOR YOUR OWN EXPERIENCE.

Gwen, I have seen too many people
waste years believing that someone else
is responsible for their happiness. That
someone else is responsible for causing
their struggle. These people have missed
out on the opportunity to experience the
beauty, and the challenge, of life. All of
the power on this earth exists in you at
this very moment and it is unlocked by
a simple decision. The decision to take
responsibility for your experience of life,
for you. Others might seem to upset you in

life, but as you experience this pain realize that this is *your* decision. No one can hurt you without *your* permission. No one can ruin your day without *your* permission. No one can make you happy without *your* permission. I am not asking you to live your life without emotion, in fact quite the opposite; live your life through your emotional experience, but never allow emotion to have absolute meaning without you getting a chance to contribute to the internal discussion. Never, ever give up this right to create the association of an emotion with a meaning that supports you and your values. This is a powerful gift that the vast majority of people you will have in your life will have chosen to relinquish. *You are responsible for your own experience.* This understanding is the greatest gift I could ever leave to another person; I hope you cherish it as much as I do.

There are many more things I am sure I will leave you, but these are good pillars on which to build a values-based approach to life. And although you are not here yet, I look forward to all of the wonderful life lessons you will be teaching *me*. I love you, Gwen. Always.

—Dad

SECTION TWO

Thoughts, Lessons, and Simple *(not necessarily easy)* Todos

AS A FATHER

"The best inheritance a parent can give his children is a few minutes of his time each day."

▷ Orlando Aloysius Battista

The reason this letter first impacted me so much was the fact that I have three kids, Grace, AJ, and Avery, who are a little bit older than Gwen. I was impressed by Bill's ability with words and secretly wished I could put my feelings into words the way Bill could. Everything he said I knew to be true, and I wanted my children to know I wanted the same for them. Over the next ten years, I would come back to this letter from time to time. I read it to Grace a few years ago when she was going through a difficult time to share with her Bill's advice that there are no shortcuts in life and that she is responsible for her own experience.

A simple todo:

If you have kids, take this letter and rewrite it, add your own advice, and give it to them. Life is too short to not live by some of Bill's wise advice. I wished I had written my own letters like this much sooner. I'm proud to say, by the time this book is published, I have finally done it and written those letters. And sad to say, it took me a decade to do it.

A REDEEMED
REGRET

*"There are no regrets in
life, just lessons."*

▷ Jennifer Aniston

Bill left us in August 2014. I miss him every day. We all
have regrets in life, and I have one regret with Bill. At
Bill's memorial service, I couldn't bring myself to say
any words. I prepared something to say and let the
opportunity pass by. I had Bill's letter to Gwen in my
jacket pocket. I knew his words would be better than
anything I could say. As I looked around the room, I
observed that Bill was survived by five very strong
women: his wife, Jess; his daughters, Gwen and Roxy;
his sister, Cris; and his mom, Kelly. In that moment I
realized his letter wasn't just for Gwen or even Roxy.
It was for Jess, Cris, and his mom. They needed Bill's
words to help guide them on this next journey without
Bill. I needed to give this letter back to Gwen. I also
needed to rewrite and address it to Jess, Roxy, Cris,
and Kelly, which I have finally done. Sadly, it took me
a decade to do it. As my mentor, business partner, and

dear friend Harvey Smith always likes to remind me, "You can always go back." Taking the courage and rewriting those letters for each of them was quite a healing exercise for me. I wish for you this same peace without regret.

A simple todo:

If you have a spouse, partner, mom, dad, brother, sister, or anyone you love, take this letter and rewrite it, add your own advice, and give it to them. Life is too short for your loved ones to not know your words of wisdom and deep love for them.

MY JOURNEY TO THIS BOOK

"It's not what you look at that matters, it's what you see."

▷ Henry David Thoreau

Every August Jess, Gwen, and Roxy celebrate Bill by releasing balloons on the anniversary of his passing. As the ten-year anniversary of Bill's passing was approaching, I began feeling the weight of my regret from not sharing his letter at his celebration of life.

In January of 2023, I committed to finally compiling this book. I sat down in my hotel room and pondered an outline and started brainstorming book titles. These titles had been swirling in my brain over the last ten years:

- A Letter from Bill

- A Letter to Grace . . . or AJ . . . or Avery

- A Letter to Your Kid

- A Letter to Someone You Love

None of these titles felt quite right. Then, as I reread the letter, the introduction *Hi Beautiful* jumped off the page. That's it. *Hi Beautiful* is the title. With deep reflection I realized I'd missed the deepest part of Bill's letter. After ten years I could finally see it. This letter was for me. I needed this letter just as much as Gwen, Grace, Roxy, AJ, Avery, Jess, Marianne, Chris, Tam, Jerry, Catherine, Bill's mom, my mom, Jess's mom, Jess's dad, my dad, and so many more people that I love.

A simple todo:

Life is too short. Love yourself; reread the letter as if it were written specifically to you.

THE FINAL MISSING PIECE

"Just as ripples spread out when a single pebble is dropped into water, the actions of individuals can have far-reaching effects."

▷ His Holiness the Dalai Lama

Embrace imperfection and share yourself, your thoughts, and your kind words with those you love. I compiled this book for you. And honestly, this book is a reflection of that advice I needed to give to myself. For far too long, I held this letter as if it were for me to keep. I held it in my jacket pocket at Bill's memorial. I held it on a blog that I never shared with the world. I never thought it was the perfect time or perfect place. Rewriting a version of this letter is a simple step to share yourself with those you love. If writing your own version of this letter is not something that suits you, then perhaps a quick conversation is more your style. That quick conversation could set a whole new path in motion for you and those you love. Don't wait for what you think is the *perfect* moment.

Say it to one person

An amazing thing happened as I began to draft my portion of this book. It started with a simple conversation as my team and I were having an off-site dinner. I mentioned to Elena, one of our team, that I was writing a book, and I shared the story of Bill and the letter to Gwen. When I heard, "That's amazing. I can't wait to read it," I felt more committed to completing it. I went back to my hotel room and began outlining and drafting all the thoughts I had been holding inside me for the last decade. I printed the draft the next morning and gave it to Elena. She then made a comment to our entire team about me writing a book. This was the first time the idea of this book was shared with others. Just one person's affirmation triggered me to finally write the first letters to Marianne, AJ, and Avery.

Six weeks later, I still had a draft and knew I finally wanted to share it. Yet, I was still holding back—holding on—just like I'd been doing all along. I then realized why I was holding back. I had never shared with Jess my desire to write the book, nor my deep regret that I didn't share the letter at Bill's memorial, and how much this letter to their daughter meant to me.

I finally took courage, connected with Jess, and shared the whole story with her. I didn't know how she would react. My biggest fear was that she would be offended or say no. Her response was quite the opposite. We were both in tears sharing our deep connection and love of Bill. We found ourselves sharing how amazing he was, how beautiful his writings and his handwriting were. Bill was still with us. Jess was overjoyed with the idea, and I sent her the draft of the book. I checked in after several weeks had gone by. Jess shared she hadn't been able to read the book just yet.

The ripple effect

A few weeks later, I headed off to a personal development retreat in the UK. For four days I was off-grid: no TV, no internet, no phone. At that retreat we did a visioning exercise, and as part of that exercise I wrote about a moment in the future where I was with my wife, Marianne, in a coffee shop when a gentleman walked up to us and thanked me for writing the book. He had a daughter and his "Hi Beautiful" letter to her changed their relationship and opened her to a whole new life. This vision fueled me to realize I needed to complete the book, not just for my family and Bill's family, but for many families.

After the retreat on my way back toward London, I turned my phone on for the first time in four days. I received a text message from Jess.

". . . Kelly is coming for a visit tonight and I
was wondering if I could share your book
with her? It's so wonderful and I can't wait
to see the final product!! [heart emoji]... I just
read Roxy the letter from Bill, some is a little
above her head but I tried to explain it in a
way she could understand. I hope his words
help her now as well as in the future, forever.
Thank you so much [praying hands emoji]"

—Jess

I was overrun with emotion and amazement. Jess had already shared this with Roxy and Kelly, Bill's mom. I realized in that moment: I couldn't stop and I didn't know how this book would even impact everyone. It wasn't going to happen in some perfect way, which had held me back for a decade. It was happening in an imperfect, beautiful way.

At that retreat I realized my biggest mistake in life was hiding—hiding myself from others. I wanted things to be perfect before I shared them. I finally realized that things would never be perfect.

My simple advice: embrace imperfection and share yourself; you never know where it might lead. It will lead you to where you are meant to be.

MAKING IT YOURS

*"You only have one life to live.
Make sure it's yours."*

▷ Eleanor Brownn

I hope you appreciate Bill's letter as much as I do. Your letter, your conversations, shouldn't be Bill's or mine. Make it yours. Share what you have learned and experienced so far in life with those you love.

Below are some questions that may stimulate your own thoughts.

- Who do you want to say *Hi Beautiful* to?

- What would you like to share with your future self?

- What do you wish you could tell a younger version of yourself?

- What's your biggest lesson in life?

- What lessons have you learned from your mentors or elders?

- What has had the most impact on you?

- What's your biggest failure, and what did you learn as a result?

A simple todo:

Rewrite Bill's letter to yourself and never forget:

▷ Lead your life based on your values.

▷ All existing means to your desired end
   are wrong.

▷ There are no shortcuts in life.

▷ Never compare your inside with somebody
   else's outside.

▷ Avoid the boring people.

▷ Never do anything solely on the assumption
   that you will be rewarded for it.

▷ You are responsible for your
   own experience.

▷ Love yourself.

▷ Embrace imperfection and share yourself.

THE SIMPLEST THING

"Life is not complex. We are complex. Life is simple, and the simple thing is the right thing."

▷ Oscar Wilde

Bill's words and my journey to share his words have emotionally impacted everyone, especially parents. In sharing this message, there was of course some resistance. I heard the comment, "Great, now I am going to have to write these letters to my kids." Yes, Bill, and I think you should!

A conversation about one of the lessons stated in Bill's letter is a great start.

I can appreciate you may desire the loving words you share to be perfect. It could take a few hours, days, or even weeks to produce the words in a way you want to share them. In the meantime, there is something you can do now. Perhaps the next time you are about to say *Good morning!* to someone you love, simply say *Hi Beautiful!* instead. Just two simple words—that's all it takes to start. You never know where it might take you or what beautiful conversations it will begin.

Hi Beautiful! What will you share today?

HI
BEAUTIFUL
JOURNAL

Use the following pages
to capture your thoughts
and ideas about saying
"Hi Beautiful!"
to people in your life.

HI BEAUTIFUL

....

....

....

....

....

....

....

....

....

....

....

....

....

....

HI BEAUTIFUL

. . . .

. . . .

. . . .

. . . .

. . . .

. . . .

. . . .

. . . .

. . . .

. . . .

. . . .

. . . .

. . . .

. . . .

HI BEAUTIFUL

....

....

....

....

....

....

....

....

....

....

....

....

....

....

HI BEAUTIFUL

. . . .

. . . .

. . . .

. . . .

. . . .

. . . .

. . . .

. . . .

. . . .

. . . .

. . . .

. . . .

. . . .

. . . .

HI BEAUTIFUL

. . . .

. . . .

. . . .

. . . .

. . . .

. . . .

. . . .

. . . .

. . . .

. . . .

. . . .

. . . .

. . . .

. . . .

HI BEAUTIFUL

. . . .

. . . .

. . . .

. . . .

. . . .

. . . .

. . . .

. . . .

. . . .

. . . .

. . . .

. . . .

. . . .

PAYING
IT FORWARD

*"When you learn, teach.
When you get, give."*

▷ Maya Angelou

For those of you who know me, you know I love the number three. Proceeds from this book will go to three places. First, to Bill's family: Jess, Gwen, and Roxy. I want to make sure the gift Bill has given me is shared with his three girls. Second, to help those surviving family members who have experienced an untimely death deal with the loss so that their loved one's spirit endures. Third, to simply help me spread this message to create and inspire love in every leader, father, brother, mom, sister, husband, wife, and partner.

ABOUT
ANDY
PAINTER

A little over two decades ago, Bill invited me on a journey, although neither he nor I realized it at the time.

Prior to meeting Bill, from the age of five, I had a passion for coding software. The process of taking a concept and creating a new reality transfixed me. For years I leaned into this skill. To the outside world, I created success. Yet something was missing. I wanted more . . . but I didn't know what *more* was. The processes and tools could only take me so far.

And that's when Bill came into my life. Bill's passion for people opened my mind to new opportunities. Through our work he held up a mirror, and his light helped me see what I'd been missing.

He showed me I could achieve a certain level of success through skill, focus, and determination, but I couldn't do it all on my own. Success only comes from the team we surround ourselves with and how we interact with the individuals.

For me, this was a challenge. It didn't come naturally. I had to learn we don't need to be perfect. We don't need to know it all. And when we release control to our team, we can have it all.

Bill's light shone brightly, and I took my first steps in a new direction.

By creating a team in the right way, Bill, our partner Steve Davis, and I achieved success beyond our wildest dreams.

And then, as we were growing the organization we'd built together, we lost Bill. His passing awakened a spark in me, something I couldn't describe at the time. About a year after Bill's passing, we sold the company Steve, Bill, and I had built. That spark continued to grow, and I had a clear vision for the future and the work that would drive me in this next chapter.

I wanted to continue our work and give leaders the tools and insights they needed to create and inspire positive change in the world.

And I knew the perfect person to partner with—my current business partner, Harvey Smith. I'd worked with Harvey as my coach for a decade. His skill of understanding people and ability to effortlessly break down the barriers of communication to create teams that perform at a high level was, and remains, unrivaled.

Together, we created Institute Success for leaders who have a desire to be better.

Being better is about having a clear vision, taking imperfect action, reflecting on the results, and having the determination to do it again. Only better this time.

It's simple, complex, and life-changing.

The journey starts with you. You don't need to be perfect. You don't need to know it all. And you certainly don't need to do it by yourself.

The first steps start with you being kind to yourself and understanding who you are as a person. Who are you at your core? What drives you? What is your vision? What is your light?

Once you have clarity on your purpose, the rest of the journey is downhill.

We often hide our lights. When you look into your mirror, you may catch a glimmer of it. Or perhaps you always knew what it was, yet events in life's journey caused you to hide it away.

Bill's light enabled me to transform my life, and the lives of thousands of leaders.

And to keep Bill's spirit alive, I'm going to invite you on a journey.

What is your light? What is your beauty to share?

Every morning, a new dawn rises. The world hands

us the gift of a new opportunity to make new decisions—and to do it better this time.

It may be as simple as the two words "Hi Beautiful" to one person.

Or it may be a manifesto that changes the world.

The real question is whether you're going to hide your light or let it shine.

Bill's memorial was on Lake Travis in Texas just before sunset. We all sat and watched the sun set that day. One of Bill's friends created a Facebook group called Sunsets with Bill, and every few weeks, someone posts a beautiful sunset and memory of Bill. Every time I see a sunset, I am reminded of Bill and his spirit. Every morning that sunset turns to a sunrise, and I am reminded that it's my turn to shine my light as bright as Bill's.

KEEP UP WITH ANDY

hibeautiful.co

@HiBeautifulBook

andy@andypainter.com

andypainter.com

linkedin.com/in/andypainter/

Printed in the USA
CPSIA information can be obtained
at www.ICGtesting.com
LVHW051700270823
756436LV00012B/598